The Waldorf Homeschool Handbook

Shine on,

Dana Ashton

The
WALDORF
Homeschool
HANDBOOK

Donna Ashton

The Waldorf Homeschool Handbook

Editor: Bernadette Emerson
Graphic Design: Roscoe Welply
Book Cover Painting: Yasmeen Olya
First edition 2013

**LCCN 2013953374
eISBN 978-1-936426-15-7
pISBN 978-1-936426-14-0**

Printed by Signature Book Printing (www.sbpbooks.com).

This book was typeset in Van Dijck.

Audrey Press
P.O. Box 6113
Maryville, Tennessee 37802

Visit us at www.audreypress.com

❊ Dedication ❊

To **Lily and Brooke** -- without whom this book would not have been possible. To my best friend and husband **David** for his support and love. And to **all the Waldorf families in my group** who cheer me on and let me know how I touch their lives.

Acknowledgements

A SPECIAL THANK YOU to Valarie Budayr who guided me into writing this book and who has encouraged and supported me from the beginning.

To the amazing team at **Audrey Press** for their dedication and ability to turn my words into this awesome book.

Also to **Yasmeen Amina Olya** for painting my imagination into the cover of this book.

To **Anne Cleveland** for all her guidance and Waldorf wisdom.

Thanks to **Carol Budzinski** for believing in me when I needed her.

A shout out to my Waldorf best-friend mama **Illya Gonzalez** who is always there to listen.

A big thanks to **Janet Alison** for her dedication to keeping me true to Waldorf and filling in the gaps.

A HUGE thanks to **all you wonderful homeschooling moms** who are on this journey. I am so grateful to be able to share my experiences and knowledge to help you navigate the roadblocks I went through.

Contents

"To see a World in a Grain of Sand and a Heaven in a Wild Flower, Hold Infinity in the Palm of your Hand and Eternity in an Hour."

~ William Blake ~

∽ Foreword ∽

The book you hold in your hands is unlike any other.
It provides you with a strong foundation of educational methodology while keeping you moving towards your homeschooling dreams in a practical way. Taking on the full responsibility of educating your child can feel exciting yet overwhelming. Take heart and know that in your hands you hold a key to not only educating your child but learning to observe and understand them in a deeper way.

Donna Ashton is your capable guide. She and I have been virtual colleagues for years, sharing conversations about Waldorf methods, parenting, and learning the ins and outs of the on-line world. We share the common goal of reaching out and connecting with you.

As a veteran Waldorf teacher and founder of Boys Alive! I have a keen interest in how boys learn. I have given many interviews, talks, and provided family coaching over the years in an effort to educate, inspire, and motivate parents and teachers to "think outside the box." While Donna Ashton's focus is both boys and girls, homeschooling and Waldorf methods, we benefit from her years of being willing to "think outside the box," too.

Donna has ably undertaken the daunting task of explaining not only the foundational philosophy of Rudolf Steiner (not for the faint of heart) but connecting it with the practical reality of your Waldorf homeschooling day. She has summarized this wise and healing education so that it is accessible to everyone.

If you are picking up knitting needles for the first time, telling a story, arranging a nature table, singing a song or playing the flute, you know you are held in friendship, and have access to the knowledge and support of Donna along with the many experts she has gathered together on a wide variety of topics – all to enable you to be a successful homeschooling family.

Many of us think about writing books but fewer actually undertake the arduous task of encapsulating and organizing many streams of ideas and information. You will appreciate Donna's efforts as she has given you the overarching wisdom you need, along with the nuts and bolts of homeschooling and how to fit it all together in your busy family life.

Not only has Donna continued to homeschool her own daughters, she has taken the time to write this book while also creating a vibrant and active on-line community in support of homeschooling families world-wide.

Donna courageously shares her journey with us. Like us, she wrestles with her own doubts, frustrations, uncertainties, and parenting challenges, allowing her readers to connect with her in a very real way. She has willingly blazed a trail so that other homeschooling families can follow her with a surer step – with more confidence, more courage, and more certainty – saving you hours of frustration and wasted time.

As the author of *Boys Alive! Bring Out Their Best*, I recognize the effort it takes to create an organized, thoughtful book. I know Donna and I share the hope that you will dog-ear these pages, spill coffee on them, and write notes in the margins… in other words: Keep it close by your side and USE IT often!

Congratulations, Donna, on providing us with a valuable reference and guide for the Waldorf homeschooling journey.

May this book inspire you and encourage you to shape your homeschool days in a way that allows you to expand your head, your heart, and your hands – bringing harmony and curiosity into your home.

Blessings on your journey!

Janet

Janet Allison
Founder of Boys Alive!
www.boysalive.com
Portland, Oregon
September, 2013

The Waldorf Homeschool Handbook

" To truly know the world,

LOOK DEEP WITHIN YOUR OWN BEING;

To truly know yourself,

TAKE A REAL INTEREST IN THE WORLD. '*

Rudolf Steiner

Welcome
to the Waldorf
Homeschool Handbook!

AS A HOMESCHOOLING MOM of over seven years, I clearly remember when I first discovered Waldorf education. I knew it was exactly what I wanted for my children. It had creativity. It had art. It had many of the things we were already doing, and it had the same belief and core values I wanted to bring to my children. Once my decision was made, I was ready to jump in with both feet. However, I didn't know where to begin. At that time, there was little information online about Waldorf homeschooling. And what I found was vague and unclear -- especially to someone unfamiliar with the concepts and the vocabulary. I felt like I was facing a jumbled mess of theories and ideas.

These days there are so many websites, blogs, and resources available; it seems to be the opposite of my early experience. Now you might feel overloaded, overwhelmed, and truly intimidated by what you find in your research. Your first reaction might be, "I could never do this!" As far as I know there is no other book out there that leads you to the information and helps you explore and establish Waldorf homeschooling in an easy, concise way. My primary goal in writing *The Waldorf Homeschool Handbook* is to explain exactly what you need as a beginner in this journey.

ꙮ MY STORY ꙮ

I found Waldorf education when my girls were three and a half. At that time, the girls were attending preschool three days a week at our local church. I had considered homeschooling since they were born and had ruminated on the idea for years. Enrollment for the following year of preschool was looming on our horizon. The next step was the four-year-old class, which meant attending every day of the week. I felt that they were not ready, and I was not ready for them to be gone so much of the time. I found myself thinking, "This is the time. It's now or never." I talked to my husband and we decided to move forward with homeschooling. I was very enthusiastic. I had never heard of Waldorf education or the Waldorf method. I didn't know anything about what I was going to do for homeschooling and I was ready to explore all of our options.

At a state homeschooling conference, I found a guide to choosing the best curriculum. I didn't find Waldorf in it, but it led me down an unexpected path. Because I like everything in my life scheduled and mapped out nicely, I assumed I would choose a method that was very organized, detailed, and rigid. When I took the quiz in the book, I was surprised to find out that methods such as Charlotte Mason and Unschooling came up for me. I realized that if I really wanted to mimic the structure of traditional school, then

I might as well just enroll them. It was a good opportunity for me to clarify what I wanted for my children. I wanted to have independent thinkers. I wanted to use the arts and music.

I hear so much these days about art programs and music programs being cut from schools. I wanted my children to have access to musical education, art, and handwork. I wanted my girls to learn information that was practical and relevant to their lives. I wanted to nurture a love of learning that would transcend their school years.

Then, by divine intervention, synchronicity, or whatever you want to call it, the summer before we began homeschooling, Waldorf came into my awareness several different times. I started researching it and that's when I knew. Unfortunately, there were no guidebooks. There were no step-by-step manuals. I only had access to general and incomplete information that I had to piece together. Luckily my children were very young, not even four, so I had time to let a lot of the ideas and techniques percolate.

So, here we are, six and a half years later. I'm currently finishing up teaching my girls the fourth grade and we're still going strong, loving Waldorf, and feeling so blessed that I found this amazing educational method to share with my children.

Now I want that same opportunity for you. I want you to feel that Waldorf-inspired homeschooling is accessible. I don't want you to give up when your children are six or seven because you're not sure what to do. A lot of people do, I think, tend to use Waldorf for the early years because they think the toys are beautiful, the materials are beautiful, and they are playing outside in nature and it's all great. And then when it's time for first grade and academics, they falter. I'm here to say that it is so worth it to push through and keep going. It's worthwhile to let your child unfold, to use a curriculum that meets your child where they are developmentally, and to see how that nurtures them and feeds their souls. And, really, that's what Waldorf education does. It feeds their body, their soul, and their mind.

Some of you may have chosen homeschooling because you want to send your child to a Waldorf school but there isn't one in your geographical area. Perhaps other factors that led you to Waldorf-inspired homeschooling are the cost of private school tuition, or having a special needs child.

It's important to note that a Waldorf-inspired homeschool setting is different than a brick-and-mortar Waldorf School. Accredited Waldorf schools have highly trained teachers who have studied Steiner's methods extensively.

A Waldorf-inspired homeschool embraces the traditions and philosophies of Waldorf education but allows flexibility as you tailor the curriculum to your child's needs. The most important point is to have a joyful experience with your children as they grow and learn in a nurturing and creative environment.

A Road Map

Thank you for joining me on this journey. I hope that this book will give you a road map. Again, I'm not here to say, "Here's how you do Waldorf," because that is the beauty and also the challenge of using Waldorf. You, as the teacher, need to digest and ingest the material so that it becomes part of you. Then you can turn around and offer it to your child in a way that is authentic to you and meets their needs at the same time. Meanwhile, you can bring your own personality and your own gifts into what you are doing. I will give you a foundation to begin, sketch out the path for you, and then you can come back with your imagination and watercolors and fill in all the beautiful parts.

Unit 1

Understanding the Basics

In this section we will look into the basics of Waldorf philosophy and how these concepts relate back to homeschooling. The Waldorf method has a rich foundation of literature and I've attempted to give you an overview of the concepts. Know that there is much more out there to explore! You will find further reading suggestions in the resources guide.

"**THE BEAUTY**

OF THE WALDORF SCHOOL

Is that it is designed entirely

TO KEEP CHILDREN INTACT

UNTIL THEY ARE READY

to move out into the world as whole individuals

Joseph Chilton Pearce

Who
is Rudolf Steiner?

What
is Waldorf Education?

IN **1919, RUDOLF STEINER** was asked by the owner of the Waldorf-Astoria Company to begin a school for the children of factory workers. The idea of setting up a school for children of working-class families was revolutionary in its day. Rudolf Steiner used the opportunity to put into practice ideas that had been evolving within him for many years. Because Steiner believed that each human being holds infinite potential, what became known as Waldorf education had the goal of educating children to have free will and full development of their heads, hearts, and hands. This can also be thought of as physical, emotional, and intellectual development.

The first Waldorf School was revolutionary for its time -- open to children from all social, religious, racial, and economic backgrounds, and co-educational. By 1928 it had grown to become the largest non-denominational school in Germany, serving as a model for other Waldorf Schools in Germany, Switzerland, Holland, England, and the United States. It is notable that Nazi Germany did not tolerate Waldorf schools and the education of "free-thinkers" and so forced them to close.

Waldorf education was created to meet the unique needs of each child and to nourish the child's body, mind, and spirit. With the idea that every child should have opportunities to try 'something of everything', the curriculum is linked to a child's developmental stage when the child is "ripe" for the subject learning and the topic is appropriate and enlivening, rather than taxing, to the child.

Rudolf Steiner divided human development into seven-year cycles. Ages 0-7 are considered the period of early childhood or the physical stage; the time when humans are growing into their body. Ages 7-14 are the heart of childhood, where children have a vivid imagination and see in pictures. Ages 14-21 is the age of adolescence, where ideas and self-discovery blossoms.

Obviously, Steiner's range of early childhood is broad. But the primary way this relates to us in the Waldorf homeschool environment is Steiner's belief that academics were not to be offered during early childhood -- until the change of teeth (losing baby teeth). (There is a lot of theory behind this, and you can find more information in the resources guide.) According to Steiner, once the baby teeth are lost and the permanent adult teeth come in, the child's access to different parts of themselves starts to change. So, during the early years, the will forces of the child are used to foster the growth of balance, movement, and the formation of healthy habits.

This leads us into understanding the basic concepts underlying Waldorf education. There are many reasons behind why we do things at certain times; fundamentally it hinges on the child's development and what they are ready to understand and need for their next stage of development.

Relating
Waldorf Theory
to Homeschooling

WALDORF is a living breathing form of education. It requires you to constantly observe your child. You, as the teacher, can then adapt your curriculum to meet the child where they are in their development. Through Waldorf education, Steiner wanted to provide an antidote to modern times and materialistic thinking. Waldorf honors the whole child -- body, mind and spirit -- through arts, music, handwork, sculpture, and movement. It educates the child's mind, nourishes their soul and meets their spirit at developmentally appropriate stages.

Waldorf honors the child by allowing them to have a true childhood through nature and playing. It protects childhood and simplicity through a rhythmic relationship with the seasons, nature, and by celebrating seasonal festivals. It also honors the child by waiting to teach academics until the child has completed their job of mastering movement and their bodies.

Understanding Why

As a parent who is planning to homeschool and use the Waldorf method, it's very important to understand these reasons. Then you'll no longer have to wonder, "Why do we have to wait until first grade or until the child turns seven before we begin teaching the letters?"

There is no specific manual for Waldorf education. Rudolf Steiner set forth a framework for the curriculum but part of his desire was that teachers make the subject matter their own based on their observations of the children before them. Your challenge, and your gift, is to take Steiner's recommendations and make them your own. Frustrating as it has been to many over the years, there are only guidelines – nothing is set in stone.

For example: In first grade we teach the fairy tales and learn about nature through stories. We teach the four math processes including stories about the quality of numbers. We also teach children to play the recorder and use their hands for knitting (but only after they've learned to fingerknit and make their own knitting needles).

Knowing the reasons behind why you're teaching each subject will make your homeschooling journey a lot easier. It will allow you to relax and not feel like you're not doing enough or doing too much. You will have confidence that you're right on track with where your child needs to be.

With Waldorf Homeschooling, we are looking at the human being in multiple ways. To further your understanding, let's start with the 3-fold development of a child's soul and the four bodies of the human.

∾3-FOLD DEVELOPMENT OF THE SOUL∾
(Head, Heart and Hands)

Rudolf Steiner placed much emphasis on three activities of the human soul: THINKING, FEELING, and WILLING. These can also be thought of as thoughtfulness, emotional development, and activities that are intentional. While children are developing ALL capacities of thinking, feeling, and willing at every age, their development is more focused on one.

∾ Development of the **Forces of Will**, age 0-7, Hands:
In the first seven years of life, the child is primarily living in the will, learning nearly everything through physical activity. During these years, learning takes place mostly through the child's imitation of the activities of adults and older children. Learning through movement comes readily to this age child. Age three is the birth of memory and "I" have my own life.

∾ Development of **Feeling**, age 7-14, Heart:
Though still active, between the ages of seven and fourteen, the child's feeling life is the strongest, and all that is taught through imagination and the arts penetrates deeply. Learning through images, feelings, pictures and stories connect to their heart and soul. Ages 7-14 is learning through polarities (opposites) and the arts.

∾ Development of **Thinking**, age 14-21, Head:
Every teen is active and emotional but now thinking -- which has been built upon the feeling and imagination plus the fostered will of the early years -- creates a balanced person. Learning through intellect, not reacting but thinking before doing. Having common sense, opinions, and rational thoughts.

✣ FOUR BODIES OF THE HUMAN ✣

Steiner believed that there were a total of four "bodies." (Not just the physical body, though that is the first one we incarnate into.)

❧ **Physical**: Our actual physical body, the part of us which is perceived by the senses.

❧ **Etheric**: Also called the Life body. You feel your energy, your child's energy, although you can't see it with your five senses. While developing the etheric body, the child is mastering his own physical body, her own ability to move in space.

❧ **Astral**: This is sometimes called the "soul body." Consciousness, independence of thinking. Having one's own perception, ideas, thoughts, decisions, and ways of behaving. This gives us our ability to have a desire and move toward meeting it (such as being thirsty or hungry and satisfying that need).

❧ **Ego (I)**: This is the most individualized yet universal aspect of our humanness. Everyone can call himself "I" but we can not call others by that name. When its home has finally been built -- the physical body, the etheric body and the astral body-- the "I" comes in to take on the consciousness of the individuality. It is the spiritual connection of why you are here.

The 12 Senses

YOU ARE, OF COURSE, FAMILIAR with the way we take in the world through five senses – sight, touch, taste, smell and hearing. Steiner understood that we have still other ways to take in the world and defined twelve senses into three groups.

❧ THE LOWER SENSES ❧

- **The Sense of Touch**: We contact the world through the organ of the skin. Tactile experiences are touches, hugs, and being held.

∾ **The Sense of Life/Sense of Well-Being**: The way that the body is working and connects with the rhythm of the world around us. This includes determining if you are tired, thirsty, and hungry.

∾ **The Sense of Self-Movement**: The ability to sense one's orientation in space and how the parts of the body are moving.

∾ **The Sense of Balance**: Physical balance, as well as balance in life, means being centered. Steiner says "Look at the sense of balance…we acquired this sense only gradually in life, we just don't think about it because it also remains in the night of consciousness."

༄ THE MIDDLE SENSES ༄

∾ **The Sense of Smell**: Relates to memory. Protect this sense during the first seven years.

∾ **The Sense of Taste**: Not only physically tasting but also knowing in an emotional way that an experience is "sweet" or "sour."

∾ **The Sense of Sight**: Our vision and the ability to distinguish color and form. Being able to study a landscape, picture, or person deeply.

∾ **The Sense of Warmth**: Children don't fully develop this sense until age nine. Our sense of the temperature of things outside of our bodies and experiencing inner warmth, too. It is the sense of nurturing, love, and joy.

❧ THE UPPER SENSES ☙
(developed during adolescence)

❧ **The Sense of Hearing**: Not only hearing the vibrations of sound through the inner ear but hearing the outer world also.

❧ **The Sense of Speech or The Sense of the Word**: Again, to hear what someone is saying, the meaning behind their words. This refers to hearing another person, not yourself.

❧ **The Sense of Thought**: Thinking things through, analyzing, expressing opinions and realizing ideas.

❧ **The Sense of Ego or the Individuality**: Who am I? What is my place in the world? Our experience as an individual and how that can bring us back into oneness with everyone.

❧ THE FOUR TEMPERAMENTS ☙

Rudolf Steiner talked about the Four Temperaments and how an understanding of the temperaments can be a tool for communication with your child. The Four Temperaments (first described by the ancient Greeks) can be likened to the four elements, and even characters such as those in *Winnie-the-Pooh* to aid in understanding their qualities.

There is a lot on the subject of temperaments available in books and online (see the Resource Guide), but here I will give a general overview.

∾ Choleric: The fire element. This is an energetic person who cannot be ignored, has high energy and makes a good leader. They can be quick tempered, but are also quick to forgive and move on. They have a purpose, they like a challenge, and must be "first."

᠅ **Character: Rabbit**.

∾ Sanguine: The air element. This is the social butterfly who flits around, has many friends, is happy and loves what is "new." They love beautiful clothes, items, and can be easily distracted by the next thing that comes their way.

᠅ **Character: Tigger**.

∾ Phlegmatic: The water element. They can be soothing, loyal, they go with the flow and are often in their own world. They like to finish what they start, but can sometimes have a hard time getting started on something new. They think deeply and act slowly. They love food.

᠅ **Character: Winnie-the-Pooh**.

∾ Melancholic: The earth element. From the earth we see rocks as solid and hard. Melancholics can be heavy in their manner, and thin-skinned and overly emotional. They are usually detail-oriented and love to sympathize with others' troubles.

᠅ **Character: Eeyore**.

There is much to learn about the temperaments and I encourage you to research your temperament as well as your child's.

Once your understand what motivates your child, you can use care to help balance the temperaments. This offers yet another perspective and way to understand your child and yourself and deepen your relationship with each other.

Donna's A-ha

It was an eye-opener to learn the traits of my phlegmatic daughter, who is so opposite from my choleric temperament. For years, I was concerned that when I asked her a question, she waited so long before answering. I wondered if there was something wrong. I was accustomed to quick answers and my other choleric daughter reinforced my impression that this was the norm. Now, after studying the temperaments, I know she is not just trying to annoy me, or doing things "on purpose"; this is how she processes information. It allows me to be patient and let her be herself. I can look at her from a different perspective now.

"**IMAGINATION** *is more important than* **KNOWLEDGE.**"

⟨ *Albert Einstein* ⟩

Some
Notable
Aspects
of Waldorf Education

❧ FIRST DO, THEN UNDERSTAND ☙

WALDORF EDUCATION fully embraces the child at each developmental stage. Traditional education has children doing much fact-based learning. Often this leads to frustration and overload because the child's brain isn't prepared to handle pure academic learning.

Through stories, music, verse, movement and art, a child first experiences information physically and soulfully. The morning lesson incorporates many different subjects all based around the same theme. Children learn their letters through movement, first by walking the shape of the letter before writing or painting the letter strokes. The letter is then reinforced through rhymes with actions, stories, and music. By first doing, children come to a concrete, tangible understanding of a concept before they are expected to apply it intellectually. It isn't that your child copies only your outer movements, but that they also experience your inner attitude of devotion, care, focus, sense of purpose, and creative spirit.

MAKE EVERYTHING INTO A PICTURE

There is great power in using imagery with your child. It enables the child to see or imagine concretely the topic at hand. For every concept taught let there be imagery. For example, when teaching the letter "T" you might have your child draw it in the shape of a tree in their lesson book. When teaching multiplication, you can tell a story about a gnome who is saving apples for winter. Each of his storage sheds holds four apples, so our gnome will need four storage sheds for his 16 apples.

Rudolf Steiner suggests that we use images to grow on. It's important that the imagery we're teaching inspires the imagination and sparks the joy and adventure in learning. Static imagery produces static thinking.

🌿 *Some Questions to ask Yourself* 🌿
as You Prepare Your Lessons

∾ Does the lesson teach ideas and concepts through vibrant images?

∾ Does the lesson provide images with which your child can grow?

∾ How do the images in one lesson relate to other areas of the curriculum?

∾ Are the days, weeks, and months organized in ways that balance thinking, feeling, and willing activities?

∾ Does your child have an opportunity to express themselves in kinesthetic (movement) ways?

∾ Are facts, ideas, and concepts taught in narrative modes of pedagogy?

∾ Do the narratives spark and ignite your child's feelings? What kinds?

⁔ RELATE EVERYTHING TO PRACTICAL LIFE ⦅

In Waldorf education learning is applied to "real" life. Each day unfolds in a predictable, rhythmic manner. In the pre-school/kindergarten years, the child is learning primarily through imitation. Most of the child's day consists of meaningful work and activities with a purpose such as cooking, baking, gardening, doing laundry, cleaning, and taking care of art supplies and the homeschool learning area.

∾ LEARNING THROUGH STORIES ∾

Storytelling seems to be a lost art, but you'll soon recognize the life it brings back into teaching and your relationship with your child. The opportunity to look into your child's eyes and gauge their feelings and reactions by watching as your story unfolds is amazing! It brings an essential part of you into the mix, which is the key to Waldorf-inspired homeschooling.

Waldorf's lack of pre-made textbooks doesn't mean your child will not get a full rich dose of literature. Children create Main Lesson Books to document their progress through drawing, painting, writing and form drawing.

∾ NATURAL TOYS & MATERIALS ∾

Waldorf encourages natural materials and beautiful surroundings. Wooden toys, silks, pinecones, acorns and other items from nature are preferred for a child to get the feel of real materials.

Art and school supplies are also high quality to give the best and truest experience. While these may cost more up front, the quality and value of these items is well worth it. We still have crayons from when my girls were four! The materials last and the wooden toys can be fixed instead of discarded. And they feel and look amazing.

It may seem daunting to acquire everything you need, but start small and work items in as you go. Make a wish list for birthdays or holidays. (See resources for websites and ideas.)

❧ WAITING FOR ACADEMICS ❧

Steiner felt that academics should not be taught until the change of teeth. A child is born with a set of teeth, but now that he is making something of his own (permanent teeth), he becomes a more grownup human being. He's on the path.

There are many physical factors that indicate a child might be ready for academics. Examples include:

❧ A child who has been living for seven spring seasons.

❧ Successfully hopping on one foot.

❧ Reaching a hand over the head and touching the opposite ear (indicating longer limbs).

These indicators all point to physical readiness. The child has had a chance to master these movements, these physical things, before starting work on the head.

❧ HANDWORK ❧

Waldorf education encourages children to develop in a well-balanced way. Handwork develops pathways in the brain, strengthening the understanding of math and expanding complex patterns and thoughts. Handwork also develops a child's sense of color, form, visual tracking, and numeracy. Knitting, crocheting, sewing, felting, cross-stitch, woodworking, and wet felting are taught as specific subjects. Each craft honors the fact that our hands are learning tools that have refined capabilities.

Handwork uses both sides of the brain. Tracking skills, for example, are greatly enhanced by handwork. Visual tracking is instrumental in developing reading skills.

As your child creates their handwork they are also developing self-reliance, creative self-expression, and a sense of caring, as many handwork projects become gifts for family members and friends.

Handwork in the homeschool curriculum integrates the head, heart, and hands to prepare your child for the world.

Children will learn knitting in the first grade. In knitting, you are creating many loops. Then you pull loops through those loops, and then you pull even more loops through those loops. Suddenly you've got a fabric. It's similar to the way you take the random thoughts that you have in your head, and put them together, and create ideas. You are formulating concepts. This is where the first grade child is.

The second grade child is usually ready to transition from knitting to crochet. A crochet hook differs from knitting in that you've got to hold it in one hand. It usually comes in more towards the middle or end of second grade to really just reinforce "This is my right hand," or "This is my left hand," and that pushing forward deciding which hand they will favor. Second grade children are testing right and wrong. They start to feel that pull and the fables, legends and saint stories fit them perfectly.

❧ BIBLICAL AND MYTH STUDY ❧

❧ **Third grade** introduces the Old Testament, where children see consequences for not listening (meeting their 9-year-change head-on).

❧ **Fourth grade** brings the Norse Myths and a time for opening children's eyes a bit more into the realities of the world. Adventure and balance is shown through these stories, and it is exactly where your 10-year-old will be. Local geography shows them there is a bigger world out there, but starts at home and slowly moves out.

❧ **Fifth grade** is the Greek Myths and study of ancient civilizations. They have crossed a bridge out of the heart of childhood and are moving into adolescence.

Unit 2

Rhythm, Schedules & Making it Fit

" WALDORF EDUCATION
Enables young people
TO BE IN LOVE WITH THE WORLD
As the world should be loved."

Marjorie Spock

What

is Rhythm?

OUR **RHYTHMS ARE YEARLY**, monthly, and seasonal... like the ebb and the flow of the tides, the waxing and waning of the moon, and the rising and setting of the sun each day. In times gone by, people lived and worked by these rhythms. Humans were used to rising with the sun, plowing fields, and planting seeds at the right time of the moon cycle. (See Biodynamic Farming created by Rudolf Steiner in 1924.)

Something that you do over and over is considered a ritual or a rhythm. Rhythm encompasses all the rituals we do. It includes everything from the smallest increments of our hours to the daily and weekly activities that make up our lives. Rituals and rhythm include waking, dressing, and preparing meals, to changing diapers, shopping, playing and sleeping.

However, we have become increasingly out of touch with rhythm and ritual as we live in houses with electricity and shop for food from the market instead of our gardens.

The ability to give children a sense of rhythm and consistency is very beneficial. Not only does it help them feel secure to know what is coming next, it helps you as the parent to create the flow of the day.

In- & Out- Breath

LIKE THE EBB AND FLOW OF A TIDE,
the rhythm in our days has an ebb and flow. This is what
in- and out-breath means.

🍂 In-Breath & Out-Breath Activities 🍂

∾ **An in-breath activity** is one where a child (or adult) comes
back into himself. Like painting or drawing, it is usually
a relaxing or quiet activity.

∾ **An out-breath activity** is something more active like
singing, running, playing, or dancing.

Even within activities, there can be an in- or out-breath. For example, a meal can begin with a quiet, meditative time and then be followed by some loud or boisterous conversation.

To create a comfortable daily rhythm, it is important to seek a balance between in- and out-breath activities. Think of a young child forced to sit for too long -- what does she need? She needs to stretch her legs, run and play. The same goes for a child who is kept in an over-stimulating situation with no "down time." He will crave quiet and rest.

When creating a daily rhythm, analyze the types of activities (either in- or out-breath). Do you have too many in-breath activities in a row? Or maybe the opposite is true and that is why your child has a meltdown before their nap?

Let's talk more about the elements you will use in creating this rhythm.

Foundational Points
of the Day

THINK OF THE FOUNDATIONAL points as the necessary elements of your daily life. These include meal preparation, naptimes, lessons, bath, and bedtime routine. Once you have these pillars in place, it will free your energy to be used for fun!

Picture this scenario: The kids are running around while you are checking emails. "What's for lunch mom? I'm hungry." Lunch? What time is it? Yikes! You were supposed to throw the laundry in and finish school lessons before lunch. Is there anything in the pantry? You're out of all the staples. Now what?!

Maybe you can relate to this situation or something similar. When we don't have a plan, and one that includes foundational points, things can easily get off track.

" *Receive the children in reverence,*

EDUCATE THEM IN LOVE,

and send them forth in freedom. "

Rudolf Steiner

Transitions

MOVING FROM ONE ACTIVITY to another is called a transition. Some children have a hard time moving smoothly, and planning transitions can help both children and adults. And, again, having a routine (a rhythm) will make the transitions go more smoothly.

Instead of yelling your child's name and telling them that dinner is ready, get into your child's world by speaking in images or using music to help transitions.

ᴥ **Sing a transition song**. There are many simple songs out there, or you can make one up. You end up like the pied piper...it works!

∾ **Use an instrument.** I use a metal triangle that I ring when it is mealtime. In using this, I get 100% response compared to the 50% I get by shouting "Lunch is ready!" You can use a recorder, piano, kinderharp, or even a regular bell.

∾ **Speak in images.** This is great especially for younger children. "The horse is so hungry; it is feeding time. Can you ride him on into the stable so he can have his oats?" By speaking in imagery, you speak to your child's world of imagination.

🍂 Sample Transition Guide 🍂

MEALTIMES: ⋆Mealtime song or blessing.
⋆Hold the child's hand and walk to the table together.
⋆Ask the child to set the table.

DINNER PREP: ⋆Have child help if possible.
⋆Have a special toy basket for that time of day.
⋆Listen to your child read aloud while you are working.

BEDTIME: ⋆Bedtime snack (warm milk and honey toast).
⋆Limit roughhousing and stimulating activities.
⋆Have children get "all ready" and in bed before the story.

∾ CREATING YOUR DAILY RHYTHM ∾

Now that you've considered your foundational points and transitions, you can begin to fill in the rest of your daily rhythm with the activities that are changeable and often fun.

Think of Rhythm in three layers: Foundational (laundry, meals, and shopping), Changeable (childrens' sports, errands, appointments, and seasonal activities) and Fun (what you love: reading, yoga, knitting).

∾ **The Foundational Layer** contains the points that anchor your day. Meals, naps, school lessons, errands, and laundry; all of those "must-do's" of the days and weeks. When creating your daily rhythm, add the foundational points in first to create a structure. You will then see the gaps in between where you can plug in the fun stuff!

∾ **The Changeable Layer** is that which is seasonal or lasts a set time, like kids' sports, swimming lessons, and gardening during the summer. This will affect your weekly schedule and of course the daily as you sprinkle in these temporary activities.

∾ **The Fun Layer** is exactly that! Your **extra** time to do all the things you have been waiting to do! It could be activities with your family, playgroups, yoga, a beach day, park time, painting, or just being outdoors in nature.

❧ FAMILY GOALS ☙

As you plan your rhythms, take time to consider your family values and goals. This is great to do with a spouse or as a family with older children. What is important to you? What activities do you want to include in your rhythm? Is being eco-friendly a priority? Volunteering? Outdoor sports?

Once you decide where you want to be, you can add family goals into your rhythm and schedule. Otherwise, it will likely never happen. You have to be proactive in this or daily life might easily swallow up your good intentions. Check your rhythms now and see where you can add in family goals.

✿ WEEKLY RHYTHM MAP ✿
TIMELINE WORKSHEET

Donna's Sample Weekly Rhythm Map

MON.	TUE.	WED.	THU.	FRI.	SAT.	SUN.
CLEANING	MUSIC	BAKE BREAD	WORK	HOMESCHOOL COOP	FAMILY DAY	CHURCH

Your Current Schedule

MON.	TUE.	WED.	THU.	FRI.	SAT.	SUN.

Do you have something every day?

Can you see a place to create an open space?

Your New Schedule

MON.	TUE.	WED.	THU.	FRI.	SAT.	SUN.

Creating
Your Daily Rhythm

CREATING YOUR DAILY RHYTHM will take some practice and refining and is always a work in progress. Use the exercise sheet below to list what your current daily rhythm looks like. After you've done this, label the In-Breath and Out-Breath activities so you get the "birds-eye" view.

O= Out-breath activity
I = In-breath activity

Where can you make adjustments in the balance?

Are you trying to squeeze too much into your day?

Do you need more structure?

DAILY RHYTHM MAP TIMELINE

Donna's Sample Daily Rhythm

TIME OF DAY	ACTIVITY
MORNING	MORNING ROUTINE (DRESS, MAKE BEDS), BREAKFAST, LAUNDRY
MID-MORNING	WALK, CIRCLE TIME, MAIN LESSON
MIDDAY	LUNCH AND CLEAN UP DISHES
AFTERNOON	FREE PLAY FOR GIRLS, DONNA WORK
MIDAFTERNOON	COME TOGETHER FOR STORY, HANDWORK, OR CRAFT
LATE AFTERNOON	MUSIC PRACTICE, MEAL PREP, BATH
EVENING	DINNER, CLEAN-UP (DISHES AND SWEEP KITCHEN FLOOR)
BEDTIME (7:30)	GET READY (JAMMIES & BRUSH TEETH), STORY WITH CANDLE, TUCK-IN
LATE EVENING	GROWN-UP TIME OR READING

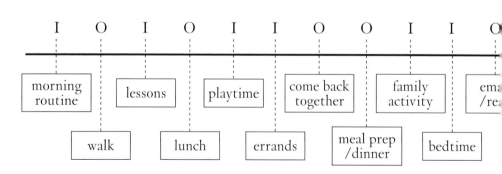

Your Current Schedule

TIME OF DAY	ACTIVITY
MORNING	_____
MID-MORNING	_____
MIDDAY	_____
AFTERNOON	_____
MIDAFTERNOON	_____
LATE AFTERNOON	_____
EVENING	_____
BEDTIME (7:30)	_____
LATE EVENING	_____

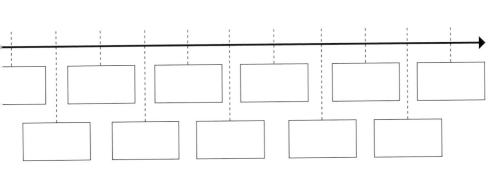

Does your rhythm need more in-breath or out-breath?

Is there free time for play and balance?

Where can you make adjustments in the balance?

Are you trying to squeeze too much into your day?

Do you need more structure?

Your New Schedule

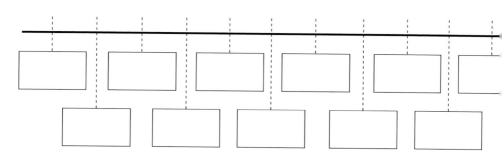

Meal Planning

THE FINAL PIECE in creating daily rhythm is meal planning. We have all been swept up in a busy day only to have mealtime descend upon us with no dinner plan in place. This may be the most stressful piece of the rhythm puzzle, as we are constantly preparing meals!

By planning ahead on a rotating schedule you create not only a meal rhythm, but also a much easier way to do your shopping and meal preparation. I like a two-week rotation of 14 meals; we have each meal twice a month. You can do a weekly rotation if that is easier, or you can create an entire month of unique meals.

Start your planning with food categories. For example:

❧ **Monday**: chicken   ❧ **Tuesday**: stir-fry   ❧ **Wednesday**: fish

Once you have categories in place, you can get more detailed or just leave it at "chicken" and decide what type of chicken that day. This rhythm needs to serve you, so do it the way it feels comfortable.

Steiner believed there was a cosmic connection between colors, grains, and the planets. In many Waldorf kindergartens, use of the planetary grains and colors are imbued into the week through snacks. You can use this approach to create a daily rhythm for your children. Use grains of the day for meals or snacks.

WALDORF EDUCATION
GRAIN OF THE DAY / PLANETARY CHART

DAY	GRAIN	PLANET	RECIPE IDEA
SUNDAY	WHEAT	SUN	MUFFINS, BREAD, PANCAKES, CEREAL
MONDAY	RICE	MOON	RICE CREAM, BROWN RICE, RICE MILK
TUESDAY	BARLEY	MARS	WARM BARLEY CEREAL, SOUP
WEDNESDAY	MILLET	MERCURY	MILLET W/VEGGIES, MILLET PORRIDGE
THURSDAY	RYE	JUPITER	BREAD, SWEDISH RYE COOKIES
FRIDAY	OATS	VENUS	OATMEAL, COOKIES, "OATLOAF"
SATURDAY	CORN	SATURN	CORNBREAD, CORNCAKES, POPCORN

You can also relate the color of the day to food. For example, you can cook and serve red lentils on Tuesday.

Kids love to know what to expect and feel secure in their daily routine.

Get creative and have fun with this!

MEAL IDEA CHART

DAY	BREAKFAST	LUNCH	DINNER
SUNDAY	OMELETTE	PASTA	CHICKEN
MONDAY	EGGS	EGG SALAD	STIR FRY
TUESDAY	OATMEAL	HUMMUS W/RAW VEGGIES	FISH
WEDNESDAY	YOGURT & FRUIT	PBJ	CASSEROLE
THURSDAY	CEREAL WITH FRUIT	SOUP W/GRILLED CHEESE	PIZZA
FRIDAY	PANCAKES	YOGURT W/GRANOLA	CROCKPOT
SATURDAY	WAFFLES	SALAD WITH FRUIT	MEXICAN

Waldorf Moms' Top Tips to having a Rhythmic Day

∼ Valarie Budayr

Each night I write down the five most important things to accomplish the following day and put it on the fridge. When I wake up I take a few quiet moments for myself. It's important to take breaks throughout the day.

∼ Jennifer Tan

A priority is planning meals and meal times on week days. You can do this on weekends and even plan to feature Steiner's grain and color of the day.

∼ Rebecca Richard

A wise woman (Kristie Burns!) once told me to have three pillars that you work your day around. For us, it is our breakfast together, our afternoon walk, and our group snuggle at bedtime. Besides that, I second Jennifer Tan's meal planning suggestion. I think having a household management binder that is nice to look at and full of all the info/lists I need inside page protectors so I can check things off and write notes with wet erase marker keeps me organized.

∼ Kristie Burns

Those three pillars or anchors are what keep me together each day! Another thing I always tell people is to have a clear goal for what you want your rhythm to feel like because even if you don't "make it" each day, you at least need something to strive for. The third thing I always keep in mind is that some days the DAY has its own rhythm. If a child got ill perhaps this is the day to learn about caregiving and compassion. If there was a snowstorm perhaps this is the day to build an igloo (it takes an entire day but is so worth it!)

Unit 3

Your Unique Curriculum & Homeschool Space

In this unit I will give you a glimpse at what homeschooling looks like. We will discuss your homeschooling space, ideas to set it up, what types of curricula could work for you and how to choose.

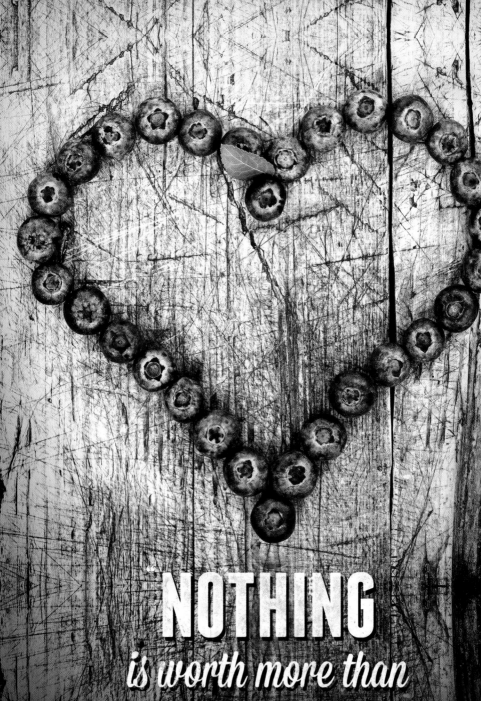

"NOTHING
is worth more than
THIS DAY."

Goethe

What
a Homeschooling Day Really Looks Like

YOU MAY BE WONDERING what homeschooling looks like and how to integrate it into your days. It can seem like a scary or intimidating path to begin, but I am here to tell you it is no such thing.

I recall my first two weeks of teaching first grade, being so nervous and unsure. Then I realized that it was just my girls and me, and our activities were very similar to what we had been doing in our two years of kindergarten. Once I came to this awareness, I felt more relaxed and confident.

Having a solid foundation was a **BIG KEY** to this easy transition, so please take the time to delve into Unit Two, where we covered rhythm. I cannot stress enough the importance of having those foundational pillars in place.

"Homeschooling" means just that -- you are schooling while living your life in and around your home. That includes the chores, feeding baby, naps, errands, and telephone calls that go on in your typical day. Homeschooling simply becomes another part of your routine.

Picking a firm time to begin school will help keep your morning flow going (and fend off time wasters like checking emails). It is so nice not to have to get up and get your child off to school early. You have the freedom to decide what works best for your family.

For the early grades (Kindergarten, First, and Second) the time it takes to complete Main Lesson, Circle Time and any other additional supporting classes like handwork and foreign language should be about two hours.

∾ OUR DAY ᵕᵉ

In our home, we typically begin school around 9 am, which gives us time for morning chores, breakfast, and our morning walk.

∾ Circle Time

We begin school with circle time, which can last anywhere from 20 to 45 minutes. In earlier grades, circle time is much shorter and only increases with more math and spelling practice. First grade circle time is about 10-15 minutes at most.

∾ Main Lesson

Main lesson can last an hour or longer depending on the grade and lesson block, but in earlier grades it might be 30 minutes. Try not to judge the effectiveness of the lesson based on time, but on the quality of what is being taught and the child's comprehension. Allow for your child's interest to expand the time of the lesson, if needed.

∾ Lunch Time

After main lesson, it is usually close to lunchtime. My girls have free play while I prepare our meal. (In the earlier days, we had a snack in between circle time and main lesson.)

∾ Afternoon

After lunch, I take time to work or do something by myself. We come together again around 3:00 or 4:00 for another school activity such as handwork, painting, crafts, or baking. When my girls were younger, the ebb and flow of activities was more frequent, adding a story time or drawing into our early afternoon. Visualize short bursts of being together alternating with their play, a rhythmic in- and out-breath.

∾ The Rest of the Day

The rest of the day and the times in between consist of working and typical homemaking tasks such as laundry, meal prep, and errands. You can see that the homeschooling day is simply life with some homeschooling mixed in.

You can incorporate homeschooling into your days by setting up your rhythm and working slowly to put these pieces in place. This took years for me to establish and get right for our family. You will need to experiment with what works best for YOU and your family. Try something different if it isn't working for everyone. Keep adjusting, assessing, and rebalancing.

⧽ WHAT TYPES OF CURRICULUM ⧼ ARE RIGHT FOR YOU?

This is a big topic and one most parents will want to figure out right away. Let's start with a few questions to help you narrow down your choices. There are many options out there for you in Waldorf-inspired curricula.

∾ 1. Time

How much time do you have to devote to planning daily/weekly lessons? Be honest here. If you only have one child, you may have time to create your own curriculum and dive deep, but if you have three, it may be a different story.

Are you working part time or do you own your own business?

Take into consideration all your regular responsibilities.

∾ 2. Your Temperament and Personality

Are you an organized person? Go with the flow? If you like details and planning, then a curriculum that has just the basic ideas may be for you. Otherwise, you might prefer something that includes detailed daily lessons plans.

∾ 3. Cost

Cost may also be a factor depending on how many grades you need to purchase. Some curricula are for a small budget, while others are a bigger investment. Check the used curriculum and supplies groups online. You may be able to sell yours back when you are through, depending on the curriculum.

I believe answering these questions will lead you in the right direction to finding a curriculum that fits.

Donna's Tip

Less is more when it comes to curriculum. Don't be fooled into thinking that two or three resources means you are more prepared. Often, curricula are conflicting in what and when they are teaching subjects during the year. Instead, I suggest one main curriculum to follow and supplement that with books and stories that fit with the plan.

You can also create your own lesson plans without buying a prepared curriculum. I did a bit of that in the early grades and then realized I was just too busy to keep going in that direction, even though I enjoyed it.

For example, you could get a few fairy tale books from the library and some nature stories and teach the letters. The four processes are taught through stories about the math gnomes or squirrels. All are very doable without purchasing a curriculum!

"One touch of natur
MAKES
The whole world ki

Shakespeare

Setting Up
Your Homeschool Space

WE TRANSFORMED our previous (rarely used) dining room into our homeschool and craft space. We love it! We have a large table with adjustable legs (from Ikea®). When the girls were younger they used stools; now we have small office chairs that adjust for height. The cabinets in the back of our space house our supplies such as painting materials, wool roving, yarn, craft supplies, and extra paper.

If you don't have a dedicated room to use, you can simply use a kitchen or dining room table, or even a desk or coffee table! You can make your schoolroom or space look however you like.

It is beneficial to have a cabinet or shelf to store your supplies and have them all in one spot. I store crayons in baskets and colored pencils in glass jars. If your school space also serves other purposes in your family, consider a rolling cart or a bookcase with doors so the materials can be tucked away when you're not schooling.

I like to make our supplies accessible to my girls. It is important that they take care of their materials and learn to clean up after each use. Storing the tools in a proper way will ensure many years of use and will help children feel confident that they can do something for themselves (and help you as the parent!)

I have a chalkboard on the wall I use for chalkboard drawings and teaching in general. You can use a moveable one or even a smaller slate. My girls use small slates to practice form drawings and math. They also have white painting boards. I bought these years ago, and they are a great investment. Ours are white hardboard, but they are made from birchwood as well. We made drawing pads out of brown grocery bags and newspaper.

❧ SOME BASIC SUPPLIES ❧

- ∾ yellow, blue, red block crayons
- ∾ yellow, blue, red Stockmar brand paint
- ∾ 1" paint brush(es)
- ∾ painting board(s) (white or birchwood)
- ∾ main lesson book(s)
- ∾ beeswax for modeling
- ∾ colored silks
- ∾ chalkboard and chalk

*Don't forget a set of all of the above for YOU as the teacher.

❧ NATURE TABLE ❧

You may use a small table or shelf (we use the end of our cabinets) to create a nature or seasonal table.

Decorate the nature table with items from nature -- found in your backyard or on hikes -- as well as wooden animals, felted or crafted items, beeswax models, small paintings, silks, and anything else you like.

I use a silk as the base in a color that reflects the season and add to it. So, for March we may use a light green silk and add a few daffodils in a glass jar along with our felted spring maiden. Then in April, we might add new blooming flowers, baby animals, and Easter eggs. In May we might switch to a sunny yellow silk and a May Day bouquet. You can change your table often or leave it the same throughout the season.

"**EDUCATING THE MIND**
without educating the heart
IS NO EDUCATION AT ALL."

Aristotle

Planning

ONCE YOU'VE MAPPED OUT your daily rhythm, planned your space, and made decisions about curriculum, it is time to delve into planning out your lessons. Whether you use a prepared curriculum or create your own lessons, you will still need a plan (and a planner) to keep yourself on track. Planning is the foundation of your homeschooling. It is a vital piece that will make or break your school year. Having a solid plan is a lot like having the pillars of rhythm in place. You may not always follow your plan exactly, but it will be the backbone of your teaching. A plan gives you the confidence that you are covering the material and an accountability of what has been learned. Of course, it is important to have flexibility to change the plan if you need to slow down or speed up based on your child, but having a plan in place will be the springboard for that.

Goals for Your Homeschool and Child

Do you have ideas, dreams and goals for what you want your homeschool to be?

Each year as I begin my planning, I write down some general homeschool goals, and what I would like to bring to each one of my girls in the upcoming year. I find it helps me maintain focus and provides reminders to add the extra spelling practice one child may require, or whatever those individual goals might be.

You can use the following reflection questions to aid you in developing your intentions.

∽ What are your goals as a teacher?

∽ Think about Steiner's 3-fold aspects of the soul.
What are your hopes for your child this year for their head, their heart, and their hands?

∽ What do you want your homeschool to feel like?

✖ BECOMING FAMILIAR ✖ WITH THE MATERIAL

Before you even begin to plan, you need to know what the upcoming year's material is all about. I recommend beginning this process in the spring (or summer) if possible. You can find a link to a list of recommended subjects and lessons per grade in the resource guide.

Start familiarizing yourself with the material by collecting books, checking them out from the library, or reading through the stories in your purchased curriculum. This is to give you an overview of what is to come, the feeling of what these stories will bring to your child, and what is actually going to be taught. We will explore this further in Unit Four: Presenting the Material, but to have an idea how to plan the year, it is extremely helpful to know what you will be teaching.

As you begin your planning, you may use the Internet as a source of inspiration and to gather ideas. I like to start by making a folder in my browser for each grade or concept and bookmark resources I find while browsing. You can find so many wonderful free stories, verses, songs, pictures, and inspiration online. Just be sure to bookmark them so you don't have to re-find that great verse you wanted for circle time! I use sticky notes in my physical books to mark resources that I regularly reference.

I use a 3-ring binder for my planner. The front and back pockets house all the loose notes and resources I print out to use for planning purposes. As I find something that will go with the main lesson blocks, I put it in the notebook for future use when I plan. It might be a recipe, song, verse, website, picture, or a list of books from the library.

By understanding what you will be teaching, you can keep an eye out for these supplements as you view blogs, books or other resources. This will save much planning time later. Start compiling now, so when it is time to plan you will have most of what you need to put it all together.

Meanwhile, make a list of supplies you will need that go along with the subject matter. For example, if you are teaching first grade, you will need knitting needles and yarn (for both you and your child).

⁂ PLANNING YOUR YEAR ⁂

When beginning to plan, think of it as "whole to parts." Start with the big picture, an overview, and then move to smaller and smaller pieces and details. You may use an online calendar, physical calendar, planner, or even a large sheet of paper labeled with the months.

∾ Step 1: Mark on the calendar which days you won't be homeschooling.

This includes holidays, vacations, spring break, and summer vacation. Check your local laws for homeschooling regulations so you know how many days of the week, month, or year are required. Now you can see what you have left to work with.

If you are new to homeschooling, you may wonder when to homeschool. Many use the traditional September through May (Northern Hemisphere) calendar. I encourage you to reflect on what would really work for your family. I know a mom who schools three weeks on, one week off, throughout the entire year. I prefer to take extra time off during our beautiful spring, and start light lessons in August when it is too hot to do much outside. Look at the weather, your rhythm and family schedules to decide. You can always change your schedule -- another beauty of homeschooling.

∾ Step 2: Label each month with a Main Lesson Block.

Example:
- ☙ **SEPTEMBER**: Form Drawing.
- ☙ **OCTOBER**: Fairy Tales.
- ☙ **NOVEMBER**: Quality of Numbers.

If you have purchased a curriculum that lays out the year, you can just copy it over into your planner. Your curriculum may have the Main Lesson blocks, but not in any particular order. Or you may be creating your own lessons. In either case you will have to determine the order.

There are no hard and fast rules here, but an evaluation of the material may reveal some natural choices. A farming or botany block would best be done during nice weather. Nature stories, man and animal, and Native American blocks are best suited for warm weather as well. Math is frequently scheduled during winter or indoor months. Saint stories would be excellent to do during holidays like St. Nicholas or St. Valentine's Day.

I suggest putting these obvious blocks in place on your calendar and then filling in the rest, considering the ease of transition from one to another. Use pencil, as you will most likely change things around once you fill in more details.

꙳ Step 3: Fill in with Weekly Topics.

Now it is time to fill in the weeks of your monthly plan.

Example: ☙ OCTOBER:

- ✦ **Week 1**: Fairy Tales: *Mother Holle* and *King Thrushbeard.*
- ✦ **Week 2**: Fairy Tales: *The Golden Goose* and *Rapunzel.*
- ✦ **Week 3**: Fairy Tales: *The Glass Mountain* and *The Queen Bee.*
- ✦ **Week 4**: Fairy Tales: *The Fisherman's Wife and The Three Brothers.*

Here you should provide some detail of what you will teach each week. If you have a curriculum with this information, then just transfer it over. If not, it is time to delve into your collection of notes and bookmarks. Make notes of any associated resources – those that you have and those that you'll need.

This process can take some time. It is hard to decide which stories to choose, as there are so many wonderful fairy tales and fables. Choose those that may resonate with your child, or stories you have enjoyed reading. Again, you have the flexibility to make changes, but this is the time to make your plans specific.

If you are planning a Math block, write down which story you will tell along with each math concept.

Example: ✎ JANUARY:

- ✦ **Week 1:** ★ Quality of numbers 1 & 2.
  - ★ Story about the Sun and *The Story of Two Eyes.*
- ✦ **Week 2:** ★ Addition.
  - ★ Stories about Addition Gnome.

∽ Step 4: Detailed Daily Plans.

It is time to create the specifics of your daily lessons. I use a weekly sheet with a summary at the top of what I will cover during the week, a place for notes and resources and then a five-day plan where I list out the details for each day.

Example:

∽ MAIN LESSON: FAIRY TALES ∽
King Thrushbeard- Letter K ✦*The Glass Mountain-* Letter M

- ⚑ Monday: ✦Tell story of *King Thrushbeard* and draw picture p. 35.
  - ✦New recorder song: *Three Blind Mice.*

- ⚑ Tuesday: ✦Re-call/tell story and write summary sentence.

- ⚑ Wednesday: ✦Tell story *The Glass Mountain* and draw picture p. 47.
  - ✦Homeschool co-op.

- ⚑ Thursday: ✦Re-call/tell story of *The Glass Mountain* and write summary sentence.

- ⚑ Friday: ✦Painting from *The Glass Mountain.*
  - ✦Bake mountain muffins.

The weekly sheet is the place to add in all the other activities you want to accompany the Main Lesson, such as recipes, songs, handwork, crafts, stories, and foreign language. This will also be the record of what you are teaching.

ADJUSTMENTS AND CHECK-UPS

Do a quarterly or semester check-up on your progress. Are you behind? Right where you should be? Do you need to modify your plan?

This is an organic plan that should have some flexibility and breathing room. Don't try to schedule so much that you can't possibly get it all done. (A common tendency, as there is so much great material we want to share!)

Be kind to yourself if things haven't gone exactly as you hoped. Learning to homeschool is a process; it takes experience to get into its rhythm.

I do an end-of-semester summary (one in January, one in May). This I keep for my records and to help me assess where we still need practice or how far we have come this year.

MONTHLY AND WEEKLY RE-ALIGNMENTS

Before the start of each block, I look through the material I will be covering and make sure I have all the supplies needed. Do I need to check out a book from the library? Get some yarn or special clay from the craft store? I mentally review what is coming and get prepared to bring that to my children.

Each Sunday, I glance at the upcoming week and refresh myself on what is coming. I may read stories again, practice my songs or new circle time movements, get baking ingredients organized or craft items prepped.

If you have a plan in place, this weekly preparation shouldn't take very long. If you haven't planned well, you may find yourself spending long hours on the weekend catching up. Most likely this will cause you stress and overwhelm that can be avoided with a well-laid out plan.

There will always be adjustments to make and new ideas that will spring up when creating lessons. I let these new inspirations in when it feels right, even if I don't use my planned lessons. If not, I have everything I need to make sure my child is getting what they should from the curriculum.

Plan, plan, plan -- then relax and enjoy!

Unit 4

Presenting the Material

It is time to take what we have been building on and start teaching what we know. Knowing our children and ourselves is a big part of this.

"PAUSING TO DELIGHT

In the simple joys of everyday lif

IS THE ONLY WAY TO TRULY LIVE."

❧ *Rachel Macy Stafford* ❧

Meeting Your Child

Where They Are

UNDERSTANDING YOUR CHILDREN has been your job since their birth. Homeschooling has the advantage of allowing YOU, the person who knows your children better than anyone else, to be the one bringing material to your children.

If you have been following along through this handbook, and building on each step, then you will already have your rhythm, homeschool space, and plan ready.

Now it is time to add the "school" component. What does this mean? We looked at a typical homeschool day in a previous unit and discovered it is a lot like daily life, with the addition of more school structure. In a homeschooling setting you have the ability to speed up or slow down the pace of lessons depending on how your child is learning.

This **meeting your child where they are** means both academically and developmentally.

For example, if you have a young first grader, they may not be developmentally ready for the cerebral function of learning to decode language. You can slow the pace down and give them more letter-related crafts, nature stories or form drawing until you feel they are ready. Likewise, you may increase the pace if your child quickly embraces reading and writing. Or you might delve deeper into a subject if it is one they love.

Meeting your child where they are is tailoring school to fit the needs of your child. If you find yourself stumbling, revisit the reflection you've done on your child's temperament and goals for insight.

Teaching Waldorf Methods

﹌ MAIN LESSON ﹌

MAIN LESSON IS THE TIME when the academic curriculum material is being presented to your child. Depending on the child's age and grade, it can vary from 20 minutes to two hours. You can choose to do the main lesson in the schoolroom setting, a living room, or even outdoors. Don't limit yourself; get creative and make it fun.

In a typical homeschool first grade main lesson, the teacher presents a chalkboard drawing and then tells a story (fairy tale) to introduce a letter of the alphabet. Then the teacher and child draw a representation of the story in their main lesson book. The next day the story is re-told back to the teacher by the child, and a summary sentence, paragraph, or letter is added to the child's main lesson book.

Most material is told through stories, especially during the early grades. Math, science, history, and geography are brought to life through wonderful stories and biographies.

☘ Tip for Learning a Story ☘

A helpful tip for learning a story: read the story three times, then make an outline of the main plot, including ideas and characters. The outline can be written or a series of quick sketches. You can use this outline if you need while telling the story. Don't worry about not remembering everything. Enjoy yourself, and your child will sense that enthusiasm.

Waldorf education also places a strong emphasis on beautiful art. Use the Resource Guide for tutorials, videos, and books that will help you develop your skills in each of the following techniques.

☙ CHALKBOARD DRAWING ❧

Get some good quality chalks and practice drawing on the board. It is a bit different from the techniques in the main lesson books. You might create a drawing and cover it with a silk, curtain, or cloth to keep the element of surprise before you begin a story. My girls loved this! The anticipation piqued their interest.

There are many beautiful chalkboard drawings in the Waldorf style online. Find some inspiration, but don't be intimidated. These techniques take practice.

☙ BLOCK CRAYONS ❧

I wasted a few years of owning block crayons before I had a clue what to do with them. I couldn't figure out how these blocks of color would somehow allow me to create the amazing Waldorf-style pictures in main lesson books, but it happened!

You only need red, blue, and yellow block crayons for a long time. Invest in these and they will last for years. I keep the yellow separated so it doesn't get other colors on it. A pad of newsprint paper (available at craft stores) is used for cleaning the crayons. We have had the same pad since first grade.

A little practice with block crayons will allow you to guide your child to create beautiful art.

❧ WET-ON-WET PAINTING ❧

Wet-on-wet watercolor is another traditional Waldorf skill that takes practice. I had never painted on wet paper before I started with Waldorf. There is so much you can experience with this painting technique. And the results are beautiful!

❧ Supplies for Painting

✦ For best results, use **high quality painting paper**.
Otherwise you may have warped paper and edges that curl and bubble. A 150 lb weight is preferable. The younger the child, the larger the paper you should use. (This applies to main lesson books as well.)

✦ **A ½ to 1 ½ inch paintbrush** is recommended.
We use 1". They may seem large compared to what you are accustomed to. This way of painting is not about the details, but the blending of color and the feeling that the colors evoke.

✦ **Stockmar paints** (red, yellow and blue only in the early grades).

✦ **A natural sponge** for smoothing wet paper and removing air bubbles.

- **A cloth** to wipe the brush and excess paint.

- **A water jar** to rinse the brush between colors.

- **A large plastic container** for submerging paper.

- **A paint board** to paint on and allow painting to dry before removing.

I mix the paint colors in large jars and leave them in the refrigerator so they are ready to use at any time. Then I decant paint into small baby food jars for each child.

∾ Instructions

- **Dip** the paper into water until submerged.

- **Remove** and place it on a painting board.

- **Smooth** the paper with a sponge.

- **Dip** a brush into water and then into the paint.

Make sure to clean the brush between colors to keep them true.

Have fun!

Remember that the colors will soften as the painting dries. Don't remove the painting from the board until it is dry. Some teachers like to round the corners of the paper for aesthetics.

Enhancing Your Skills

WHAT GIFTS DO YOU BRING to your homeschool? Perhaps you are a musician, or already knit or speak a foreign language. Are you a great baker, cook or mathematician? Consider where you have skills that can support your homeschool teaching.

I played the flute in school, so it was relatively simple to pick up a recorder and teach my girls with only a little preparation. But my math skills are another story. My husband has strong math skills so I use him for support. I am re-learning math the Waldorf way and I find that math makes more sense to me this time around.

Take this time before you begin schooling to learn a new craft or hone your skills. You only need to learn what you will teach in the upcoming year. Take it bit by bit; one step at a time. You will build on your skills as you go. For a kindergarten-aged child, work on the basics of painting, drawing and finger knitting. Then you can add knitting and recorder for first grade.

☙ TROUBLESHOOTING HOT SPOTS ❧

You may need some help in your homeschool if there is a skill you wish to bring to your child, but for whatever reason you can't or you don't have the time.

Check with your homeschool group, co-op, friends, or family. Maybe a friend who speaks Spanish teaches a class at her local co-op. A local music teacher might give lessons to a homeschool group. There are endless possibilities, and you don't have to do this all by yourself!

If there is something you are having trouble with, (maybe storytelling or painting) ask for help from a friend or seek out more resources online. These basic concepts may feel foreign to us. Some of us haven't painted since we were in grade school! It's okay to feel uncomfortable when trying new things.

Unit 5

Self-Care, Support & Community

You've made it this far and should have started the steps of creating your homeschool. This next piece of the puzzle may be the most important one -- supporting yourself and getting the support of your family and friends.

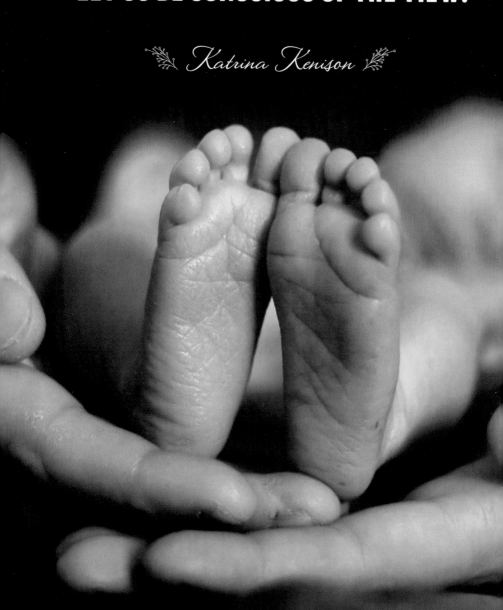

WE ARE THE WINDOWS

Through which our children first see the world.

LET US BE CONSCIOUS OF THE VIEW."

Katrina Kenison

Inner Work
What is it & Why do I need it?

ONE OF THE PRACTICES that will get you into a balanced mindset and center you is self-care. Our society is filled with things we 'do' each and every moment of our day. Creating a specific time to practice mindfulness or self-care can be helpful in so many ways. Though you are preparing to homeschool your child, the material in the Waldorf method comes through you. How you show up is a key piece.

> "You have NO IDEA how UNIMPORTANT is all that the TEACHER SAYS or does not say on the surface, and how IMPORTANT what HE himself IS as teacher."
>
> -Rudolf Steiner-

There is a lot going on in your household. Homeschooling means you are spending a lot of time within your home. You have a lot of moving parts in your life. Your children are always there, and your teaching job is 24/7. It is okay to desire time alone, especially during years with young children. Our children are sharing our energy constantly and we need to replenish it.

If we give too much without giving back to ourselves, the resulting imbalance will impact everyone in our family. Practicing self-care will help to refill your tank, rekindle your passions and excitement for teaching and living. You begin to feel worthy and loved as you celebrate caring for and honoring yourself.

As a more relaxed parent, your communication with your children is improved. Your children see and feel the effects of you being more relaxed in the environment.

HOW DO I DO IT?

What is it that really inspires you? Dancing? Music? Yoga? Painting? Writing?

The key is to find something that works for you and rekindles your passions. Having a passionate activity is the quickest way to refuel your soul.

Before my girls were born I discovered I loved gardening. It was like a secret gift I never knew about until we had our first house (and a yard that I quickly turned into gardens). My green thumb seemed to come naturally and I couldn't get enough of having my hands in the soil. I could spend hours tending my plants without realizing the time had flown by.

Fast forward to my life as a mom with twin babies and you can probably guess that by year three, my gardens were overgrown and full of weeds. About that time I realized I needed that part of myself again. I reached back out to nature, and it answered. When I spent just 20 minutes clipping flowers or transplanting seedlings, the effects were amazing! I was relaxed, calm and happy. I returned to my day a reenergized mom.

❧ WHERE DO I FIND THE TIME ☙ FOR SELF-CARE?

From my own experiences, I find that consistent time set aside every day is the most beneficial. A specific time set aside each day will help create consistency and less "forgetting."

∽ Morning
You are fresh and already relaxed, and therefore you can quickly carve out 5-10 minutes. Take a soothing hot shower. Drink a cup of tea while journaling. Perform a morning yoga routine. Or perhaps get into nature with a ten-minute walk while planning the upcoming day's schedule.

> ### ❧ Donna's Tip ❧
> I suggest getting up before your children if possible. This is time to collect your thoughts before the kids coming running in. Years ago, I would get up and meditate. Currently, I walk one morning and swim at the gym on alternate days. These precious moments are a gift to YOU.

∽ During the Day
Find small moments to come back to center and breathe. It could be while washing dishes, cooking, lighting the candle for a meal or even while washing your hands. Pick something you do often as a chance to relax and focus on the present.

❧ Evenings

I also recommend getting the children in bed early-- enough to have some time in the evening to talk with a partner, read, craft, relax or reflect on the day. You might do some journaling about your day, gratitude, or reflect on what your child needs from you.

In all these ways you carve small moments to go within. These activities that support you will evolve with you and your journey.

❧ OTHER NOTES ABOUT BALANCE ❧

❧ Boundaries

Parents may not realize that boundaries are a big issue in their lives. I'll bet there are several areas in your daily life that bleed into each other, and it is hard to tell where one stops and another begins. When we begin homeschooling, maintaining boundaries becomes even more valuable.

Perhaps you have never thought about boundaries in this way. It may take some time to look at your day and schedule and see what could be a boundary issue.

Another clue about boundary challenges is that they're often happening when we feel we HAVE to say yes, even when we want to say no. I am not referring to laundry or diaper changes; this is more about extra things that get put upon us in an unconscious way.

It is up to YOU to define your boundaries with family and friends. Parents have many roles to fill, and it is hard to balance them. Establishing firm boundaries can help prevent you from feeling exhausted and burned out.

❧ Confidence

It is hard to go against the grain from what everyone else is doing, especially in that 4-5 age range when your friends' children are going off to preschool and learning to read.

So, my best advice is to pick the path that speaks to you and is best for your family. Stand firm in your decisions and give yourself time to see the results.

Family Support

FAMILY, most likely your partner, will be your biggest influence. If you are single, then there may be an ex-spouse or mom or sister. They can be your biggest cheerleaders and supporters because they are close to home. But a lack of understanding between you and your family can cause obstacles to successful homeschooling.

The most important step in getting the support of your family is being sure that they are well informed! Your family should understand what you are planning and why. Just as you have spent time researching, reading, and looking at blogs, your family needs to understand the theory behind Waldorf education and why it works. Therefore, you need to be confident enough in your understanding of Waldorf education to explain the foundations to them.

From my own experience: Things were going smoothly, with my husband the first few years but as our children reached six years old and were still not learning to read or doing math, the questions began to arise.

The questions weren't just coming from my husband. My mom and sister began questioning the children's education. I clearly remember, a holiday when my sister was visiting and she took my girls into the other room and started grilling them about their letters!

So, why is family support so crucial? If it is your spouse or partner, it can be a deal-breaker for homeschooling. It is ideal if your partner is supporting you during this journey. I recall the first time I overheard my husband telling someone else that I homeschool and that we used Waldorf methods. I listened to him talk about all the great things the girls have been learning and how they can knit, sew, craft, and play instruments. It felt really good to hear that. He doesn't always say that to me, but just knowing he supports me and understands feels good. I feel supported.

There are also specific lifestyle choices we make as Waldorf homeschoolers, such as natural toys and playthings, limited or no media, radio, screen time, and simplicity in activities and schedules. All of these choices affect your family.

Of course, sometimes compromising is necessary. I wanted to get rid of our television, but my husband did not. So we compromised; no television until the girls are in bed. We came up with this decision together. If your partner feels involved in the decision-making, you will have more support.

Keep your family in the loop with what is happening. After homeschooling begins, they will continue to ask questions (this still happens for me!). Your spouse might appreciate a weekly or monthly progress discussion. Share what you have been doing and learning.

If a family member has skills in a particular area, bring them in to teach! You may be surprised how many great suggestions your family will have to help you with your lessons.

Family Recap

1. Help your family understand what you're teaching and why.

2. Make joint decisions and compromises if possible.

3. Keep your family informed on progress.

Once you have your family's support you will see that everything feels more relaxed.

"LET PARENTS BEQUEATH TO THEIR CHILDREN
Not riches, but
THE SPIRIT OF REVERENCE."

Pop-Culture
and Waldorf

❧ HOW **NOT** TO ISOLATE ❧ YOURSELF WHEN LIVING A WALDORF LIFESTYLE AND HOMESCHOOLING.

THIS **TOPIC IS HUGE,** and we could have a book about this alone. I believe knowing what you will and will not compromise on is a good starting place. One example is when my girls go to a party. I normally don't allow a lot of sweets and sugar, but it is unavoidable out in the world. So, they know they may have a cupcake or cake, but must drink water instead of soda or juice. I feel that they don't need added sugar, and they know now to ask for water.

You can't control what is going on at others' houses, only at your own. You can set a standard for what is done, and when your children are away from home, decide what compromises might be made. Maybe you won't let your children watch television at a friend's house, but they can watch an approved movie.

My feelings are that if you have a good foundation at home and a solid rhythm, an occasional diversion from that will not do harm. It also depends on the age of your child. I know that I am more flexible now that my girls are ten than I was when they were only five.

Again, it is about boundaries and creating a foundation. Now, when my girls see or experience something different or odd to them, they come back and tell me. These situations give me an opportunity to talk with my children about our values. If they were younger, it's a chance to re-establish our boundaries.

In your own home, when others visit you have more control over the activities and food. Perhaps your house is the only one in the neighborhood that has outdoor games in the evening or hopscotch and jump rope. You can be the place all the children like to go to really play. Like Mrs. Piggle Wiggle's house!

Having like-minded friends can be a huge blessing as there are fewer things to navigate and you can relax a bit. So where do you find these people?

Playgroups
and Co-ops

A **LOCAL HOMESCHOOL CO-OP** is a wonderful place to start even if your child is not yet school age. You can go check it out and see if any families mesh well with yours. Many families will have younger siblings to play with your child.

A co-op is usually a weekly meeting of a homeschool group at a church or other public space where classes are taught by parents, professionals or teachers. Meeting once a week or once a month is a wonderful way to get your children playing with others and more importantly --YOU talking with someone else!

If you can find other families that are also using Waldorf education, that is ideal! You can share ideas, resources, do festivals together, create a handwork group or host a parent book study.

I have a very good friend who I meet when she is in town, which is very rejuvenating. We always give each other ideas, advice, and compare what is going on with our kids. It is such a helpful lifeline.

Sometimes you have to be proactive. Ask your friends, check at a holistic moms network, attachment parenting group, La Leche League, or your local organic market. Check with your local library, where homeschoolers will definitely be.

By creating support you give yourself the opportunity to ENJOY homeschooling and feel like you are part of a tribe, a community.

Festivals

FESTIVALS CAN BE A WONDERFUL way to connect with other families. Having a larger group will create a synergy that can make your festivals a celebration! Invite neighbors and friends to participate. Even if they are not Waldorf families, they can be a part of your special event. Sharing responsibilities of a festival alleviates one person from having to do it all. You also bring the talents, energy, and gifts of others into your festival.

Seasons and Festivals are such a fun way to share in traditions and celebrate the changing of the year. The four main turning points are Autumn Equinox, Winter Solstice, Spring Equinox, and Summer Solstice. Aligning your child with the cyclical rhythms of nature is a gift you can give beginning in their early years. Your entire kindergarten can be based on nature, seasons and festivals!

There are many to choose from, but the key is to start with just a few. If you have never celebrated a festival before, take some time getting familiar with what it represents. What ideas do you want to bring and tell stories about? What songs feel right to you to sing?

I created a Festival Notebook in which I placed hard copies of songs and recipes, verses, and stories for the festivals we celebrated each year. Once I had this, the next year it was easy to repeat the festival, building on the foundation I'd created by adding or modifying elements.

Some festivals will resonate more with you than others. Start with what you know or are drawn to. You are the key to the festival, and the energy you bring will be reflected in the overall feeling of the day. If possible, find other families to assist you in planning and carrying out a festival. Perhaps have several families contribute food, music, or entertainment.

When I first started creating festivals I felt strange saying verses and telling stories. I remember thinking "I hope my family doesn't think this is too weird!" But now it seems natural and they notice if I skip something. Each element becomes part of a tradition.

After trying out a few different festivals, we chose the ones that resonated with us. There are many festivals during the busy holiday season, so choose only one or two and let that be enough. You can try a different one the next year. Take this from someone who did ALL the festivals the first year and was exhausted by Three Kings Day!

❧ COMMON WALDORF FESTIVAL DAYS ❧

❧ Michaelmas: (Sept.29) - The feast of St. Michael, who is known as the conqueror of the dragon with his starry sword. Michael gives us strength to slay the dragons of materialism and egoism. You can feel a change in the air. It is a time to harvest what was sown in the spring and what grew all summer. The earth is beginning to contract as we prepare ourselves to go inward for the coming winter.

ༀ **Samhain: (Halloween Oct.31)** - Halfway between the equinox and solstice, Samhain is the beginning of the season of "dark."

ༀ **Martinmas: (Nov.11)** - The feast of St. Martin. The most famous legend of St. Martin's life is that he once cut his cloak in half to share with a beggar during a snowstorm to save the beggar from dying of the cold. Traditionally this festival is celebrated with a lighted lantern walk and singing, lighting the way through the dark nights of this time of year.

ༀ **St. Nicholas: (Dec 6)** - My girls' favorite! There is a lot you can read about this festival, as in European countries St. Nicholas is the bringer of gifts. Put your shoes out Dec. 5th and in the morning treats and trinkets fill them.

ༀ **St. Lucia: (Dec.13)** - This is the feast day for St. Lucy on which the eldest girl wears a crown of candles, a white gown and a red sash. She serves breakfast for the whole family. We had a lot of fun with this!

ༀ **Advent: (Nov and Dec)** - Advent begins four Sundays prior to Christmas. It is the coming preparations for the Christ child.

ༀ **Winter Solstice/Yule: (December 21 or 22)** - The birth of the Sun is the shortest day of the year, after which the sun starts shining longer each day. The winter solstice is my favorite festival!

ༀ **Candlemas/Brigid: (Feb. 2)** - Marks the growing presence of the sun and when the candles were made and blessed for the year. (Also Groundhog Day in the U.S.)

ༀ **Spring Equinox: (Mar 21 or 22)** - On this first day of spring, day and night are equal. We always plant our spring garden and wheatgrass for our Easter baskets.

∾ Easter: (March or April) - Easter falls on the first Sunday after the first full moon after the vernal equinox. Coloring eggs and celebrating with a hare or rabbit is always fun. Nature is waking up and everything is new and reborn.

∾ May Day: (May 1) - May Day may be best known for its tradition of dancing around the maypole and crowning the Queen of May. In ancient times, it was considered the first day of summer (thus Midsummer being mid-June).

∾ Summer Solstice/Midsummer Night: (June 21 or 22) - The celebration of Midsummer's Eve (St. John's Eve among Christians) was from ancient times a festival of the summer solstice. Some people believed that golden-flowered midsummer plants, especially Calendula, and St. John's Wort, had healing powers and therefore they picked them on this night.

✌ SIMPLE FESTIVAL TEMPLATE ✌

∾ Choose your festival, read about it, and familiarize yourself with the purpose, history, and mood of it. Is it light and joyful, solemn and reverent, busy and bright, calm and subtle?

∾ Experience the seasonal expression of the time of year. Go out and play with your child, notice what you feel, see, hear and smell. Bring some of that rich sensory experience back home with you in the form of natural objects, such as stones, branches, moss, acorns, berries and flowers. Display these in a prominent place to be enjoyed daily, and be sure to leave some on the nature table.

∾ Choose a time to celebrate your festival, invite friends and family, or keep it simple with just your household.

◕ **Celebrate by sharing a story, song, poem or verse** related to the festival.

◕ **Make a craft** related to the festival, and use the craft in an activity related to the theme.

◕ **Share simple seasonal beautiful food**.

◕ SAMPLE FESTIVAL ◕

Here's an example of how to celebrate Martinmas, an Autumn festival, using the template.

◕ Martinmas is celebrated mid-autumn as the light dwindles and we move toward the darkest days of the year. The mood is one of reverence and of connecting with our own inner light.

◕ Martinmas occurs during cool days, when the wind is blowing, colored leaves are falling, walnuts are scattered in the yard, and apples are falling off the trees.

◕ Nuts and leaves can decorate the nature table, perhaps with a little wooden fox and rabbit.

◕ Martinmas is wonderful celebrated in the early evening with family.

◕ We tell the Story of St. Martin, and sing "This Little Light of Mine."

◕ Our craft is making lanterns with colored tissue paper, glue, and little mason jars with wire handles. We put a tea light in each lantern and walk outside at dusk, each person carrying their own little light.

◕ Finally we share a simple meal of soup and bread and then deliver some soup to a neighbor or friend in need of a little light in their lives!

"Don't cry because it's over,
SMILE BECAUSE IT HAPPENED

 Dr. Seuss

Final Words

THIS HANDBOOK WAS WRITTEN to help support you on your Waldorf homeschooling journey. I want you to know that you are not alone. Those of us who are a bit farther down the way are lighting the way for you. It is my deepest passion that you discover the joys of embracing Waldorf. If I can make that journey easier, then I have been successful! Waldorf Homeschooling is an amazing opportunity to offer your child. You may experience your own personal transformation as well. I discovered early on that Waldorf is a way of life and not just a type of education or curriculum we are using. It is a living, breathing way of being. I invite you to embrace it and discover its Magic.

SHINE ON,

Donna

About the Author

Donna Ashton is the founder and CEO of The Waldorf Connection, an online resource that provides workshops, courses, and training for homeschooling families all over the globe. She is committed to delivering confidence, clarity and support to moms seeking to educate their children in a Waldorf-inspired, conscious way.

Donna has worked with hundreds of families in her core programs, Waldorf Homeschool U and Living the Waldorf Life, and through The International Association of Waldorf Homeschooling. Donna also offers a yearly Homeschool Expo and live events. After deciding to homeschool her three-year-old twin girls, she immersed herself in studying and living a Waldorf-inspired life. From her curiosity and struggles with finding easy-to-digest, practical information, she started her business in 2010 to ease the way for others.

Donna provides training, advice and resources to over 6000 families worldwide. To get started with the very basics of homeschooling, download her Starter Waldorf Homeschool Toolkit at thewaldorfconnection.com.

⌁ Contributors ⌁

Janet Allison is an author, educator, and coach working for more than a decade to advocate for boys and their success in school and in life. She speaks nationally and internationally and consults virtually - Boys Alive! educates, motivates, and inspires parents and teachers to more deeply understand how boys learn, play, and relate from a science-based perspective.
Contact her at janet@boysalive.com
www.boysalive.com

Renowned artist **Yasmeen Amina Olya** created the lovely and soulful cover for *The Waldorf Homeschool Handbook*. An accomplished musician, composer, folk harpist, and soprano vocalist, Yasmeen Olya is also a Waldorf alumna who has contributed her breathtaking illustrations to the Waldorf community for the past 15 years. You can connect with Yasmeen on her Waldorf-inspired site wisesophia.com or her official site yasmeenaminaolya.com.

Resource Guide

General

- Association of Waldorf Schools in North America ➜ www.awsna.org
- The Waldorf Connection ➜ thewaldorfconnection.com
- *Rhythms of Learning: Rudolf Steiner Lectures* - Rudolf Steiner & Roberto Trostili (SteinerBooks, 1998).
- *Understanding Waldorf Education, Teaching from the Inside Out* - Jack Petrash (Gryphon House, 2002).
- *Steiner Education in Theory and Practice* - Gilbert Childs (Floris Books, 1991).
- *Waldorf Education: A Family Guide* - Pamela J. Fenner & Mary Beth Rapisardo (Michaelmas Press, 1999).

∾ *The Essence of Waldorf Education* - Peter Seig (SteinerBooks, 2010).
∾ *The Kingdom of Childhood: Introductory Talks on Waldorf Education*
  -Rudolf Steiner(SteinerBooks,1995) ➜ steinerbooks.org/research/archive/
  kingdom_of_childhood/kingdom_of_childhood.pdf
∾ *The Child's Changing Consciousness as the Basis of Pedagogical Practice*
  -Rudolf Steiner(SteinerBooks,1996) ➜ steinerbooks.org/research/archive/
  childs_changing_consciousness/childs_changing_consciousness.pdf
∾ *Practical Advice to Teachers* - Rudolf Steiner (SteinerBooks, 2000).
  ➜ steinerbooks.org/research/archive/practical_advice/practical_advice.pdf

Anthroposophy

∾ **What is Anthroposophy?** ➜ waldorfanswers.org/Anthroposophy.htm
∾ **The Anthroposophical Society** -
  ➜ www.goetheanum.org/Anthroposophical-Society.336.0.html?&L=1
∾ **Anthroposophical Society in North America** ➜ www.anthroposophy.org
∾ **Anthroposophy E-Course with Dr. Rick Tan** -
  ➜ www.littleacornlearning.com/ecourses

Art and Handwork

∾ **Chalkboard Drawing** ➜ www.chalkboarddrawing.org/
∾ **Handwork Techniques** ➜ www.syrendellacademy.com/
∾ *Coloring with Block Crayons* - Sieglinde De Francesca
  (Spiral-bound, 2007).
∾ *Paintings & Drawings in Waldorf Schools* - Thomas Wildgruber
  (Floris Books, 2012).
∾ *Painting in Waldorf Education* - Dick Bruin, Attie Lichthart
  (AWSNA Publications, 2004).

Child Development and Parenting

- **Family Mission Statement** (from Simple Mom)
  → simplemom.net/back-to-the-basics-create-a-family-mission-statement/
- *You are Your Child's First Teacher* - Rahima Baldwin-Dancy (Ten Speed Press, 2012).
- *Simplicity Parenting* - Kim John Payne & Lisa M. Ross (Ballantine Books, 2010).
- *Heaven on Earth* - Sharifa Oppenheimer & Stephanie Gross (SteinerBooks, 2006).
- *Beyond the Rainbow Bridge: Nurturing Our Children from Birth to Seven* - Barbara J. Patterson (Michaelmas Press, 1999).
- *Boys Alive! Bring Out Their Best!* - Janet Allison (Booklocker, 2010).
- *Healing Stories for Challenging Behaviour* - Susan Perrow (Hawthorn Press, 2008).
- *Encountering the Self: Transformation & Destiny in the Ninth Year* - Hermann Koepke & Jesse Darrell (SteinerBooks, 1989).

Communities

- **The International Association of Waldorf Homeschooling (IAWHS)** - → thewaldorfconnection.com/waldorfassociation/
- **Homespun Forum** → homespunwaldorf.com/wordpress/
- **Waldorf in the Home** → www.waldorfinthehome.org
- **The Waldorf Connection Fan page** - → www.facebook.com/thewaldorfconnection
- **Waldorf Homeschool U Facebook Group** - → www.facebook.com/groups/139921892856528/
- **Holistic Moms Network** - find a chapter - → www.holisticmoms.org/category/connect/local-chapters/
- **Miss Marsha's Yahoo Group** → groups.yahoo.com/group/waldorfhomeeducators/

Curricula, Training, and Educational Resources

- **Waldorf Essentials** → waldorfessentials.com
- **The BEarth Institute (Earthschooling)** -
  → earthschooling.info/thebearthinstitute/
- **Live Education** → www.live-education.com
- **Christopherus** → www.christopherushomeschool.org/home.html
- **Waldorf without Walls** → www.waldorfwithoutwalls.com
- **The Milennial Child** → www.millennialchild.com
- **Oak Meadow Curriculum & School** → www.oakmeadow.com
- **Lifeways** → www.lifewaysnorthamerica.org/
- ***Waldorf Student Reading List*** - Pamela Johnson Fenner & Karen Rivers (Michaelmas Press, 1999).
- **Waldorf Homeschool U** → thewaldorfconnection.com/waldorfu/
- **Living the Waldorf Life** → thewaldorfconnection.com/livingwaldorf/

Early Childhood

- **Little Acorn Learning** → littleacornlearning.com/
- **Heaven on Earth** → www.ourheavenonearth.net/
- **Simplicity Parenting** → www.simplicityparenting.com/
- **Fairy Dust Teaching** → fairydustteaching.com/
- **The Practical Magic of Early Childhood** -
  → thewaldorfconnection.com/practicalmagic/

Festivals and Food

- **Little Acorn Learning Festival Ebooks** -
  - ➔ littleacornlearning.com/themebooks.html
- *All Year Round* - Ann Druitt (Lifeways) (Hawthorn Press, 1997)
- *The Children's Year: Seasonal Crafts and Clothes* - Stephanie Cooper (Hawthorn Press, 2006).
- *Festivals, Family & Food* - Diana Carey and Judy Large (Hawthorn Press, 1982).

Guidance and Inspiration

- **Parenting Passageway** ➔ theparentingpassageway.com
- **Rhythm of the Home** ➔ rhythmofthehome.com
- **The Magic Onions** ➔ themagiconions.blogspot.com
- **Waldorfmama** ➔ www.waldorfmama.typepad.com

Music

- *Come Follow Me Vol.1 and Vol. 2* (CD) - Lorraine Nelson Wolf (Ribbon Hill Music, 2005).
- **Naturally You Can Sing** ➔ www.naturallyyoucansing.com/books/
- **Home Music Making** ➔ homemusicmaking.blogspot.com
- **Music Through The Grades** -
  - ➔ www.lifebalanceforteachers.com/musicthroughthegrades.html
- *The Mood of the Fifth* - Nancy Foster (WECAN, 2013).
- *Waldorf Songbook* - Brien Masters (Floris Books, 1987).
- *The Second Waldorf Song Book* - Brien Masters (Floris Books, 1993).
- *A Day Full of Song: Work Songs from a Waldorf Kindergarten* - Karen Lonsky (WECAN, 2009).
- *Music Around the World for Recorders* - Michael Preston (Spiral-bound, 2005).

Rhythm

- ✑ *Rhythm & Organization: How to Manage Your Time, Simplify Tasks, & Align with Your Family Values* - The Waldorf Connection
  - → thewaldorfconnection.com/ebookrhythm/
- ✑ Steiner's Grain of Day Thoughts on the Cedar Ring Circle Blog -
  - → cedarringmama.wordpress.com/2011/08/26/meal-planning-grain-of-the-day/
- ✑ Ultimate Waldorf Homeschool Planner -
  - → www.lifebalanceforteachers.com/waldorfplanner.html
- ✑ 4 Steps to Rhythm Home Study -
  - → theparentingstudio.com/home-study/

Rudolf Steiner

- ✑ Rudolf Steiner Web → www.rudolfsteinerweb.com
- ✑ Rudolf Steiner Archives → www.rsarchive.org
- ✑ Rudolf Steiner Audio → www.rudolfsteineraudio.com
- ✑ Rudolf Steiner Wikipedia → en.wikipedia.org/wiki/Rudolf_Steiner
- ✑ *Soul Economy: Body, Soul, and Spirit in Waldorf Education* - Rudolf Steiner (SteinerBooks, 2003).

Lessons, Verse, and Stories

- ✑ Waldorf Library → www.waldorflibrary.org/books
- ✑ Free Stories → www.mainlesson.com/
- ✑ Sparkle Stories → www.sparklestories.com
- ✑ *A Journey through Time in Verse and Rhyme* - Heather Thomas (Floris Books, 1998).
- ✑ *Child's Seasonal Treasury* - Betty Jones (Holon, 2012).
- ✑ *Waldorf Book of Poetry* - David Kennedy (Living Arts Books, 2012).

- ***The Waldorf Book of Animal Poetry*** - David Kennedy (Living Arts Books, 2013).
- ***Tell Me a Story*** - Louise DeForest and Deborah Grieder (WECAN, 2009).

Supplies, Toys, and Crafts

- **A Child's Dream** ➡ www.achildsdream.com/
- **A Toy Garden** ➡ atoygarden.com
- **Bella Luna Toys** ➡ www.bellalunatoys.com/
- **Cedar Ring Circle** ➡ stores.cedarringcircle.com/StoreFront.bok
- **Earthsong Fibers** ➡ www.earthsongfibers.com
- **Meadow Sweet Naturals** ➡ www.meadowsweetnaturals.com/
- **Paper, Scissors, Stone** ➡ www.waldorfsupplies.com
- **Syrendell** ➡ syrendell.blogspot.com/
- **Waldorf in the Home** ➡ www.informedfamilylife.org/
- **Waldorf Inspired Learning** ➡ www.waldorfinspiredlearning.com/

Temperaments

- **The Temperaments** ➡ www.openwaldorf.com/temperaments.html
- **Steiner's Temperament Lectures** -
  ➡ wn.rsarchive.org/Lectures/FourTemps/ForTem_index.html
- **Temperament Quiz** -
  ➡ www.writing.com/main/quiz/item_id/1145443-Temperament-Test
- ***The Temperaments and the Adult-Child Relationship*** - Kristie Burns (Lulu, 2010).
- ***The Four Temperaments*** - Rudolf Steiner (Rudolf Steiner Press 2008)
- ***The Temperaments in Education*** - Roy Wilkinson (Rudolf Steiner College Press, 1994).

Quotation References

∾ **(Foreword)** - William Blake, *Auguries of Innocence* (Circa 1803).

∾ **(Introduction)** - Rudolf Steiner, *Verses and Meditations* (Rudolf Steiner Press, 2004). Verses given by Steiner between 1906 & 1925 to individuals and for group occasions.

∾ **(Chapter 1)** - Joseph Chilton Pearce (Author of *The Magical Child*) *A Humanist Talks About Waldorf Education*, in *WALDORF EDUCATION, A FAMILY GUIDE 82* (Pamela Johnson Femmer et al., eds., 1992).

∾ **(Chapter 4)** - Albert Einstein, *Cosmic Religion : With Other Opinions and Aphorisms* (Covici-Friede, 1931).

∾ **(Chapter 5)** - Marjorie Spock (teacher, poet and inspirer of Rachel Carson's Silent Spring, that led to Earth Day), author of *Teaching as a Lively Art* (Rudolph Steiner Press,1985).

∾ **(Chapter 8)** - Rudolf Steiner & Robert McDermott, *New Essential Steiner: An Introduction to Rudolf Steiner for the 21st Century* (SteinerBooks, 2009).

∾ **(Chapter 11)** - Johann Wolfgang von Goethe (Circa 1796).

∾ **(Chapter 12)** - William Shakespeare, *Troilus and Cressida* (1602).

∾ **(Chapter 13)** - Aristotle (Circa 328 BC).

∾ **(Chapter 14)** - Rachel Macy Stafford (2013) → www.huffingtonpost.com/rachel-macy-stafford/the-day-i-stopped-saying-hurry-up_b_3624798.html

∾ **(Chapter 17)** - Katrina Kenison, *Mitten Strings for God: Reflections for Mothers in a Hurry* (Grand Central Publishing, 2002).

∾ **(p. 77)** - Rudolf Steiner, *Curative Education: Lecture 2* (1924) → wn.rsarchive.org/Lectures/CuratEducat/19240626p01.html

∾ **(Chapter 19)** - Plato, *Laws, Book V* (Circa 360 BC).

∾ **(Final Words)** - unsourced yet often attributed to Dr Seuss (Theodor Seuss Geisel, children's book author from 1937 to 1990).

A YEAR IN THE
SECRET
GARDEN

VALARIE BUDAYR & MARILYN SCOTT-WATERS

 AudreyPress

HAVE YOU EVER WANTED TO VISIT THE SECRET GARDEN ?

NOW YOU CAN.

UNLOCK THE SECRETS OF THIS CLASSIC TALE MONTH BY MONTH FOR AN ENTIRE YEAR.

CRAFTS * RECIPES * GAMES

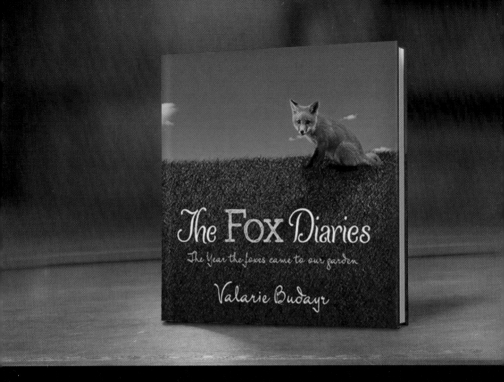

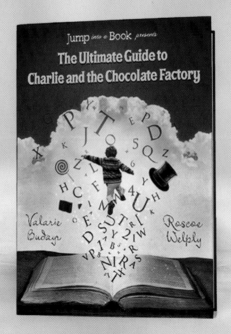